T0286327

TIME *for* KiDS

KID REPORTER

FIELD GUIDE

by **Hannah Holzer**

PENGUIN YOUNG READERS LICENSES
An imprint of Penguin Random House LLC, New York

First published in the United States of America by Penguin Young Readers Licenses,
an imprint of Penguin Random House LLC, New York, 2024

TIME for Kids © 2024 TIME USA, LLC. All Rights Reserved.

Visit us online at penguinrandomhouse.com.

Library of Congress Cataloging-in-Publication Data is available.

Manufactured in China

ISBN 9780593754955   10 9 8 7 6 5 4 3 2 1 TOPL

Design by Hsiao-Pin Lin

. . . .

Photo credits: Cover: Getty Images: (hand holding microphone, wired microphone) Valeriy
Matveyev/iStock; (marker, pencil) vladwel/iStock; (microphone with stand) Svetlana Larshina/
iStock; (notebook) Lightcome/iStock. **Interior: Getty Images:** Endpapers, 1, 81: Valeriy
Matveyev/iStock; 5: Flash vector/iStock; 7: RLT_Images/DigitalVision Vectors; 8: simonkr/E+;
13: monkeybusinessimages/iStock; 16: South_agency/E+; 18, 74, 98: bortonia/DigitalVision
Vectors; 20: Iana Kirianova/iStock; 22: Feodora Chiosea/iStock; 25: calvindexter/DigitalVision
Vectors; 27: SpicyTruffel/iStock; 30: nortonrsx/iStock; 34: Jitalia17/E+; 36, 84: vector/iStock;
38: Vertigo3d/iStock; 40: traffic_analyzer/DigitalVision Vectors; 41: gheatza/iStock; 44: vgajic/
iStock; 46: Misha Shutkevych/iStock; 47: Enis Aksoy/DigitalVision Vectors; 48: San Francisco
Chronicle/Hearst Newspapers via Getty Images/Contributor/Hearst Newspapers; 52: BananaS-
tock/BananaStock; 55: Rudzhan Nagiev/iStock; 56: Thapana Onphalai/iStock; 58: Enis Aksoy/
DigitalVision Vectors; 59: vector/iStock; 62: FG Trade/E+; 64: JakeOlimb/DigitalVision Vectors;
68: Teekatas/iStock; 72: SeventyFour/iStock; 82: aldomurillo/E+; 88: George Marks/Retrofile
RF; 90: bortonia/DigitalVision Vectors; 91: (typewriter) SlothAstronaut/iStock; 92: WWD/Con-
tributor/Penske Media; 93: CSA Images/Vetta; 96: Comstock Images/Stockbyte; 99: Maria
Petrishina/iStock. **Wikimedia Commons:** 43: Mary Garrity, public domain; 91: (Nellie Bly) H. J.
Myers, public domain; 94: Peabody Awards (CC BY 2.0)

CONTENTS

INTRODUCTION

A good journalist is curious. They ask questions and search for answers. They notice the world around them and enjoy talking to and learning from other people about all sorts of things. If this sounds like you, you might have a future as a journalist.

So what is a journalist? A journalist is someone who attempts to answer a question or explore an issue by gathering research, interviewing experts, and looking at it from all sides. Once information has been gathered in the form of written text, audio recording, video, or pictures, journalists publish their final product—which should always be factual, engaging, and easily understood.

Vocab word: A journalist is **PUBLISHED** when their work gets posted online or is printed somewhere, such as in a newspaper or magazine. What kinds of stories would you be excited to publish if you were a journalist?

What are journalists interested in? Well, just about everything!

We write about sports; food; local, national, and global events; education; technology; politics; and more. We tell people what's trendy and recommend new podcasts, movies, and music. Some journalists, like me, even get paid to write down our opinions. Many journalists (also called "reporters") have an assigned beat: a specific topic they research and write or talk about.

I'm Hannah Holzer, and I work at the *Sacramento Bee*. It's a newspaper that covers news, sports, opinions, and politics in California's capital city. Its newsroom is constantly abuzz with reporters working on stories about

Hannah Holzer

a variety of topics. The reporter on the "breaking news" beat, for example, has to be ready and willing to run out at a moment's notice to the scene of a wildfire, the office of a politician who has just announced their resignation, or a zoo to cover the birth of a baby giraffe. Breaking news reporters have to be ready to go at any time—sometimes even in the middle of the night!

Meanwhile, in a different part of the newsroom, a food reporter gets to eat at new restaurants and write about whether they liked the food. Elsewhere, a columnist is writing an opinion piece on a recent vote taken by the city council or on legislation signed into law by the governor.

All of these beats are important to readers who want to know more about the world around them.

Jobs in the field of journalism can look very different. A journalist can be someone who talks about world events on a podcast, takes pictures or videos at a grand

opening, writes about sports for a newspaper, or interviews community members on a TV or radio station.

A journalist can also be a student who writes for a school newspaper or appears on a campus television program. Student reporters often write about issues or events that impact their school campus. They might write a review of a school musical, interview teachers or professors about the classes they teach, conduct a poll among students

about the best food on campus, or investigate the shocking disappearance of a school mascot.

(Reminder: Student journalists should always put their schoolwork first!)

If your school doesn't have a newspaper, online

publication, or other outlet to publish your work, you can start your own. Ask an adult to help you.

By getting involved with your school's publication or creating your own, you can begin to inform your friends, family, and community about the topics and issues that matter most to you.

Ben Stern took an interest in the news during the COVID-19 pandemic. At that time, when Ben was only 6 years old, he started his own newsletter to keep his family informed about the latest news.

In 2022, when Ben started at a new school, he learned that one of his classmates had created a school newspaper.

"I already liked journalism and wanted to collaborate through shared interests with others," Ben says. "It gave me a great opportunity to make new friends. And I was chosen to be an editor because of my dedication to the paper. I was so happy, because I always wanted to write for others."

The school newspaper has a teacher mentor who Ben says "teaches us interesting journalism concepts, like fact-checking." Ben's favorite subject in school is writing, and he says his favorite story has been a piece he wrote and reported about "hidden spaces" on his school campus.

"I've gone to see the basement of the administrative

building [and the] garage under the school gym," Ben says. "It's been cool to see all of that, because not every student gets to see it."

After learning of an opportunity through TIME for Kids to be an official TFK Kid Reporter, Ben jumped at the chance.

"I thought, 'Hey, maybe I could do that,'" he says. As part of the application, Ben had to interview sources and write a detailed, fact-based article. He chose to interview and write about his school's physical education teacher. She's a football player on a semiprofessional team.

The fourth grader says he was ecstatic to be chosen as a TFK Kid Reporter for the 2023–24 school year. When we spoke via Zoom, Ben was wearing the official red-and-white TIME for Kids T-shirt given out to these young star reporters.

Ben's first assignment as a TFK Kid Reporter was to interview 8-year-old Julian Lin. Julian ran a lemonade stand in New York City's Central Park to raise money for residents of Maui, Hawaii, who were affected by a series of wildfires in 2023. For his next assignment, Ben got to visit the Smithsonian's National Zoo, in Washington, DC, to write a story about the zoo's three pandas just before they were to be returned to China in late 2023. Ben even got to interview the zoo's official "panda team" for the piece.

Ben's words of advice for kids his age interested in journalism?

"Anyone can become a journalist," he says. "It just takes a lot of hard work and dedication."

• • •

TFK Kid Reporter Ben Stern reports from the Smithsonian National Zoo, in Washington, DC, in 2023.

Remember: Whether a journalist's work reaches one person or a million people, their work matters.

So what makes a journalist a journalist? No matter what topic they write about, all journalists share a common goal: pursuing the truth. Some journalists, such as Bob Woodward and Carl Bernstein, whom you will learn about in chapter 8, spend years trying to uncover the truth about certain events that have been kept secret. After interviewing hundreds of sources, Woodward and Bernstein finally published the truth about a political conspiracy so serious that it forced the president of the United States, Richard Nixon, to resign from office.

"Pursuing the truth" is a big concept. What does it actually involve?

Let's say you're interested in finding out more about a bake sale that's being held to raise money to buy new books for the school library. Where should you start on your story? First, ask your teacher or a school administrator who is helping to organize the bake sale. Then contact the person or group organizing the bake sale to set up an interview. Next, you'll want to interview classmates who plan to attend the bake sale, as well as your school librarian. Of course, you should plan to attend the bake sale to take note of

what's being sold, how many people are in attendance, and what the atmosphere at the event is like. After the bake sale, you should ask the event organizers how much money was raised and what books will be purchased.

Tip: Journalists must try to be as fair as possible in their coverage. It is important to consider all sides of a story, and to report on it truthfully.

In 2021, TFK Kid Reporter Lucy Sandor tackles her dream assignment, reporting from New York Comic Con.

> **Vocab word: COVERING**—or **TO COVER** a story—means to report on or give attention to a specific topic (to provide coverage). What topic would you like to cover first?

In this book, you'll learn how to do five different types of journalism:

1. News coverage
2. Opinion writing
3. Reviews
4. Sports coverage
5. Features writing

But first, let's dive into some journalism basics.

CHAPTER I

INTERVIEWING

One of the most important skills to have as a journalist is the ability to interview people.

Tip: As a reporter, you should aim to interview at least three people for every story you write. You never know whether a source (or "interviewee"—a person being interviewed) might give you an exciting new piece of information that changes the entire focus of your story.

How do you find sources? Sources are the people you interview whose knowledge and opinions will shape your story. They are typically people with special or expert knowledge of your story's subject matter, such as teachers, politicians, scientists, or doctors. These types of sources provide expert opinions because they're knowledgeable about the topic you're reporting on. But you should always strive to also include the opinion of at least one "regular" person, who might not be an expert on your topic. For example, if you're writing about the unusual disappearance of butterflies in a community garden, you'll want to interview an expert on butterflies about why the butterflies are disappearing. You might also interview a neighborhood resident who enjoys visiting the community garden about their thoughts on the disappearance of the butterflies. Both perspectives are important.

Make sure to research the people you're interviewing before you talk to them. If you come to the interview knowing something about them, you'll have more time to ask interesting questions. Also try to get a good understanding of what you're writing about before talking to a source. Ask yourself what you already know about the topic, as well as what you need to know.

EXAMPLE STORY

Let's say you're writing a story for your school paper, the *Excelsior Gazette*, about a new reptile exhibit at the Lee Mur Zoo. Who should you interview? Lee Mur Zoo employees, local reptile experts, and community members who plan to visit the new attraction.

After visiting the Lee Mur Zoo's website with help from an adult, you find a staff directory page that lists the zoo director as Ms. Ellie Phant. Listed next to Ellie's name is her email address. Use this contact information to write to her and request an interview.

From a trusted adult's email account, draft an email to Ellie. It's important to be respectful when contacting a potential source. Address them by their full name or by using their preferred honorific, if you know it. It's also appropriate to use their professional title when applicable, such as "Dr." or "Professor."

Tip: Always immediately tell your sources that you're a reporter so they know that what they say might be published!

EXAMPLE EMAIL

Dear Ms. Phant,

My name is [Your first and last name] and I'm a journalist at the *Excelsior Gazette*. I'm writing a story about the new reptile exhibit at the Lee Mur Zoo, where you serve as director. I'm hoping to set up a time for an in-person interview, a video interview, or a phone call to talk about the new exhibit. I'm available on Monday and Wednesday after 3 p.m., or before 6 p.m. on Saturday. Please let me know if you have time to speak with me.

Thank you,

[Your first and last name]

Ellie responds to your email and says she can meet you at noon on Saturday at the front entrance of the zoo.

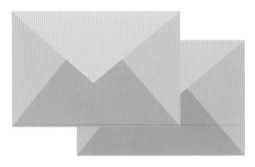

Now what? It's time to prepare for your interview. First, learn all you can about the new reptile exhibit from the zoo's website. Look for announcements about the exhibit as well as recently published news stories about the exhibit or the Lee Mur Zoo. Based on your research and the information you've collected about your topic (the reptile exhibit), prepare a list of questions to ask your source (Ellie).

Prepare at least seven questions ahead of your interview. The best questions to ask are those that cannot be answered with a simple yes or no. For example, rather than asking Ellie if she likes working at the zoo, ask her what she likes most about her job there. Framing your questions in this way will result in more thoughtful answers from your sources.

Prepare for your interview by writing your questions on a piece of paper, or by printing them from a computer. Bring them along with you, as well as a notebook and pens or pencils.

You might choose to record your interview using a phone or recording device. Then you can listen back to the interview later, as you're writing your story. Even if you choose to record your interview, you should take detailed notes.

Tip: You must ask for your source's permission to record the interview. In some places, asking permission is the law!

EXAMPLE QUESTIONS FOR ELLIE

1. May I record our interview? (If Ellie says yes, turn on your recording device now.)
2. How long have you worked at the Lee Mur Zoo?
3. Why do you like working with animals?
4. What is your favorite animal at the zoo and why?
5. Which animals have visitors been most excited to see in the new reptile exhibit?
6. How long will the reptile exhibit be open to the public?
7. Where did the reptiles that will be included in the exhibit come from?
8. Can visitors take photos of the reptiles?

Tip: Ask your source to spell their first and last name for you and tell you their exact job title. It's important to get this information exactly right.

Make sure you ask your sources all the questions you prepared, and don't hesitate to ask follow-up questions. If your source doesn't give you a detailed answer, ask questions like "Can you say more about that?" or "How do you feel about that?" If you don't understand something

your source has said, ask them to explain it.

Always end an interview by asking your source if there's anything they'd like to add. For example: "Those are all the questions I have prepared for you, but is there anything else you want to talk about?" Also ask if they'd recommend anyone else you should speak to for the article.

Remember: Always thank your source for their time.

You've conducted three interviews for your story. Now what? Review your interview notes or listen back to your recordings. Highlight sentences and phrases that you think are particularly interesting or well-stated. You may want to feature these quotes in your piece.

Beginning to write an article can be intimidating. There are ways that you can prepare. Start by reviewing all of the information you've gathered. You can star or highlight quotes or facts that seem especially important.

It can also be helpful to talk to your friends and family about what you've learned. Telling them the story can help you begin to organize and clarify it in your head.

Now it's time to write!

When writing a journalistic story, a good way to start is by using the inverted pyramid structure. This method covers the most important details up front before moving to the more specific details.

When using the inverted pyramid structure, your first paragraph should answer six questions: Who? What? When? Where? Why? How?

EXAMPLE FIRST PARAGRAPH

The Lee Mur Zoo is opening a new reptile exhibit on August 17 that will feature 34 reptile species, including snakes, lizards, geckos, and turtles. Ellie Phant, director of the zoo, said visitors will pay $6 to visit the exhibit, with profits going to benefit the zoo's reptile conservation efforts.

Who? Ellie Phant
What? A new reptile exhibit
When? August 17
Where? Lee Mur Zoo
Why? To fund reptile conservation efforts
How? Tickets purchased by zoo visitors

Think about which of the six questions is the most important part of your story. A story focused on one person will have WHO as the most important question to answer. For a story about an event, WHAT and WHERE may be

more important. Try to answer this question first.

Now that we have established all the most important details in our first paragraph, let's include a quote from one of our sources. Look back at your notes and choose a quote that you think works well at this point in your story. A good quote will say something you couldn't say better yourself.

EXAMPLE

"I have been working at the Lee Mur Zoo for 14 years, and I have never been more excited about an exhibit," says Ellie Phant. "I can't wait to see how our visitors react to Terry, the 300-pound tortoise."

When introducing your sources, give your reader an image of who this person is and why they're relevant to the story. For instance, let's say you interview local reptile enthusiast Liz Ard. How would you introduce her in your story?

EXAMPLE

"The new reptile exhibit is going to be incredible," says Liz Ard, a local architect who describes herself as "a reptile enthusiast." Ard's favorite reptile is the leopard gecko, and she has read 52 books about geckos.

TFK Kid Reporter Lino Marrero conducts a video-call interview with college basketball coach Mike Krzyzewski, also known as Coach K, in 2023.

If you are quoting from a source, you must put their words in quotation marks. That signals to readers that these words are not your own but were spoken by someone else.

Quotes must be 100 percent accurate, meaning they reflect exactly what your source said in your interview, word for word.

Quotes can be on the shorter side. Using more than a sentence or two of a quote may make your story harder to read. Choose quotes that give your story a boost. The best quotes give readers information in a way the writer could not have written better themselves. And remember to identify the speaker of the quote. If you've already introduced the speaker, you can just use their last name.

Tip: When presenting a quote, use simple speech verbs such as *he said* or *she asked*. Avoid stronger speech verbs such as *exclaimed* or *cried*—unless someone really yelled out the words!

Make sure that you've incorporated all your sources in your story, that you've included every quote you wanted to use, and that you've given your readers all the information they need.

Remember: Read over your work. Try reading the story out loud or taking a break and coming back to it with fresh eyes. This can help you make sure your writing is clear and easy to read. Look out for sentences that are too long or words that are too complicated. Try not to repeat words too often, especially within a sentence or paragraph.

Journalists almost always use the active voice. Instead of saying "Terry the tortoise is watched by zoo director Ellie Phant," try "Zoo director Ellie Phant watches Terry the tortoise."

Congratulations! You've written a news article!

Reporter's notebook: Why use one? Good reporters know the value of carrying a pen and notebook at all times. Whether writing down quotes during an interview, taking notes while covering a sports game, or jotting down thoughts while watching a ballet performance, a reporter's notebook always comes in handy.

If you were the reporter assigned to cover the new reptile exhibit at the Lee Mur Zoo, you could use your notebook to write down details to incorporate into your story. How many people were at the zoo on the day you visited? What was the weather like? What are the smells and sounds of the zoo? Instead of describing the scene as "a busy day at the zoo," try to write in more detail. For example: "It was a perfect 75-degree day at the zoo without a cloud in the sky. Dozens of happy families with ice-cream cones were crowding around the lion enclosure."

More details paint a much fuller picture for the reader. Readers love details, so make sure you write down as much about your surroundings as possible. Always have a notebook ready to go!

Vocab word: To **PLAGIARIZE** means to pass off someone else's words or work as your own. Journalists must never plagiarize. It's extremely important to name your sources and give other writers credit for their work. You can do that by putting someone's words in quotations or giving them credit by writing "according to" and the names of the writer and publication.

In 2021, TFK Kid Reporter Tabitha Kho interviews Dr. Rochelle Walensky in Atlanta, Georgia. Dr. Walensky led the US Centers for Disease Control and Prevention at the time.

CHAPTER 2

NEWS

When you think of journalism, you probably think of news reporting. That's because "the news" can be so many different things. It can be about local, national, or international events. It can be about everything from a pizza shop that just opened in your neighborhood to the president of the United States meeting with the prime minister of New Zealand. Other examples of news stories might be your state's governor signing legislation into law, a hurricane bringing heavy rain to the East Coast, NASA discovering a star, your school's new free lunch program, a species of frog thought to be extinct being spotted in Canada, or your mayor declaring May 14 Blueberry Muffin Appreciation Day.

In 2024, TFK Kid Reporter Audrey Owolo reports from the White House Press Room, in Washington, DC.

Now that you know how wide-ranging news coverage can be, it's time for you to report the news!

First, choose a topic you're interested in writing about.

Here are questions that might help you choose the subject of your news story: Is your school making any big changes right now? How far along is the progress on a new business or playground under construction in your neighborhood? Are there any local businesses that have recently opened or closed? Has your mayor made any recent proclamations? Have any awards been given to classmates, community members, or local sports teams?

If you're still having trouble choosing a topic, read a local news outlet or watch a local TV news station (with an adult's permission and guidance) to get inspiration and learn about what's happening in your community.

Assignment I

Write a 450-word article about
a news topic you are interested in.

Step 1: Choose your topic.

Step 2: Write down questions you have about your topic.

Step 3: Conduct research on your topic at the library or online.

Step 4: Make a list of three to five people you want to interview for your story.

Step 5: Schedule your interviews (they can be in person, on video, or by phone) and prepare your questions.

Step 6: Write your first paragraph, addressing Who? What? Why? When? Where? How?

Step 7: Add your quotes.

Step 8: Read and then reread your story (you can also ask a relative or teacher to read your story and give you advice).

There are many different forms of news reporting, including breaking news reporting and investigative reporting.

A breaking news reporter must be ready at a moment's notice to run to the scene of a tornado, drive to city hall, attend a news conference, or jump on the phone with local law enforcement to get details on a robbery. These reporters work quickly, interviewing sources and writing up stories in hours or even minutes.

Investigative reporters, on the other hand, might work on a story for months or even years. They act as detectives, investigating missing money in government budgets or looking into unexplained events. (Why are fish falling from the sky? Why do all the dogs in a certain neighborhood start barking at 7 p.m. every Tuesday night?)

In the 1890s, Black journalist Ida B. Wells began an investigation into violent and racist acts being committed against Black men in the southern United States. She discovered that innocent Black men were being accused of crimes they did not commit. These men were sometimes killed because of these wrongful accusations. Wells's published reporting brought attention to these horrible injustices. Despite the truth of Wells's reporting, she faced threats for writing it.

Wells was determined to bring attention to the issues affecting her community. According to the *New York Times*, Wells "pioneered reporting techniques that remain central tenets of modern journalism." That means that reporters today are still influenced by the way that Wells reported. All investigative journalists aim to be brave truth-tellers.

Tip: Investigative journalists often request information by filing official requests under the federal Freedom of Information Act (also known as FOIA, pronounced like "foy-uh"). National Sunshine Week occurs every March in the United States. It celebrates the public's guaranteed access to public documents. Ask an adult to help you look online or visit a library to learn more information about FOIA requests.

Ida B. Wells

CHAPTER 3

OPINION

Unlike news reporters, and unlike most other journalists, opinion writers incorporate their personal opinions in their stories. Non-opinion journalists are neutral in their writing, which means they don't take sides or voice their opinions.

If a city council were debating whether to approve a permit for a playground or pizza parlor on a plot of empty land, a reporter would simply report the facts and interview sources on both sides of the debate: those in support of the playground and those in support of the pizza parlor. But an opinion journalist covering the same story would take a side and argue for it.

And while reporters should remain neutral by not placing themselves in their stories, opinion journalists might use *I* statements or write about themselves. (For example: "While I do love pizza, our community needs more playgrounds, so I think the city council should approve the playground.")

Opinion journalists must still adhere to the strict ethical and moral standards expected of all journalists. So how do these writers balance their opinions with the facts?

Opinion journalists must conduct significant research for every story they write to make sure their opinions are rooted in truth and backed by facts. They also use

A mural for Wide Open Walls created by Jorit Agoch in 2019.

data, statistics, scientific research, and expert opinion to strengthen their opinions and arguments.

Before they begin writing, opinion writers do research to inspire and inform their piece. This research helps them decide on their story's angle.

Vocab word: An **ANGLE** is a story's approach. When writing a story, a journalist will consider what angle to take. The angle has to do with the story's point of view, or perspective.

For example, each year, the city of Sacramento, California, puts on an annual mural festival called Wide Open Walls. Since 2016, hundreds of large, vibrant art pieces have been painted on city buildings by local artists. This effort is funded by members of the community as well as by nearby universities, organizations, and businesses.

Opinion columnist Robin Epley thinks other cities should make their streets more colorful by investing in public art. She plans to write an opinion column for the *Sacramento Bee* calling for just that.

To write this column, Epley will need to conduct research on the Wide Open Walls event and look into how the organization receives its funding. She'll talk to Sacramento city leaders about funding for public art. And

Photos, videos, and drawings can be journalism, too.

Photojournalism: Powerful photos and videos can sometimes tell a story better than words can. Photojournalists capture stories by documenting events in a single image or video. Often the most powerful stories combine visuals (such as photos or videos) and written or spoken words (such as news articles or TV news segments), allowing readers to get a fuller and more accurate picture of an event or issue.

Editorial cartoons: Unlike other cartoons that typically serve as sources of humor or entertainment, editorial cartoons are a form of opinion journalism. Editorial cartoonists draw compelling imagery, like the faces of politicians or the scenes of news events, to express their opinions. These cartoons might depict a politician saying something they didn't actually say, to make a point. Readers know that, unlike photojournalism, editorial cartoons are not facts: They are exaggerations of events that express the artist's point of view. Sometimes all you need is a powerful drawing to make a point.

she'll research whether the state or federal government gives grants (money for specific projects) to cities to pay for art projects.

In this case, Epley's angle would be: More cities need more public art.

Typically, an opinion piece includes a "call to action": a demand that a person or group act in a certain manner. For instance, in Epley's piece about public art, her call to action could be: "More cities should invest public funds on public art projects because it makes residents happy and makes towns more beautiful."

As an opinion writer, Epley has her own opinion column. That means that when she publishes a column, it runs with her name and photo so readers know whose opinion they're reading. She's also a member of her newspaper's editorial board. This is a group of writers and editors who discuss and debate relevant issues and then decide what opinion they, as a group, are going to present on a given topic.

For example, every election season, Epley and her colleagues interview all the candidates for office in their city, county, and state. After the editorial board interviews all the candidates running for a given position, the group has a thoughtful discussion to decide which candidate they all like best. Then they endorse that person. This means the board writes an editorial—a collaborative piece that expresses the views of the newspaper, as determined by the opinion staff—to tell readers why they like one candidate better than the rest.

MAKE YOUR VOICE HEARD!

Many print and online news publications offer readers a chance to be published in their opinion pages. Readers can express their opinions in one of two ways.

Op-ed: An op-ed is a piece of writing typically between 500 to 1,000 words that's written by someone arguing their stance on a topic. Examples of op-eds might include a politician asking the public to support a piece of legislation they have authored; a student writing about the importance of picking up trash and not littering; or a doctor writing to encourage readers to wash their hands during flu season.

Letter to the editor: A letter to the editor is usually between 100 to 200 words and is a direct response to an article or column that has already been published. Sometimes, readers disagree with a publication's reporting—maybe a fact is missing or an issue is being overlooked. Other times, readers might really enjoy a certain piece of reporting and want to commend the journalist responsible for the piece. These letters, which might express criticism or congratulations, are then published by the news outlet.

Assignment 2

Write your own 150-word letter to the editor.

• • •

Step 1: With an adult's permission, choose a newspaper, news magazine, or online news outlet.

Step 2: Read three articles of your choosing.

Step 3: Of the three articles, choose one you especially enjoyed or found interesting. Why did you like or dislike it? What did you learn? What opinions do you have on the subject after reading the piece? Take some time to think about what you've read and form your own opinion.

Step 4: Write your thoughts in a letter of no more than 150 words.

Step 5: Ask an adult to help you find an email address or online form to submit your letter to the publication.

You have an opportunity right now to get your name and opinions published. If your first letter isn't published, don't give up! Keep reading the news and forming your own opinions on different topics. Practice writing, and keep submitting letters and op-eds.

• • •

CHAPTER 4

REVIEWS

Critics are journalists who write opinion-based reviews. Whether they're watching a movie, eating at a restaurant, listening to an album, or seeing a play or dance performance, critics are tasked with telling readers about their experience.

Often reviewers use a rating system to score their experience. These scores, which are usually out of five or ten points, are similar to the grades you get in school. These grades represent the reporter's opinion, but the reporter should try to remain open-minded until making their final judgment. For example, a food critic trying a new restaurant might not like the appetizers but might love the main courses and desserts. That critic should give the restaurant a mostly positive review because they liked most of the dishes.

Being a critic comes with a lot of exciting opportunities. Experienced review writers get to see upcoming movies or go to new restaurants before the public has access to them. They get to go early so they can share their opinions on the new thing before anyone else. If a reviewer has a positive opinion about a new movie or a new restaurant, it might encourage readers to buy a ticket or make a dinner reservation.

Sometimes, readers will disagree with a critic's opinion. It is important that critics stay confident and do not let these disagreements discourage them from writing their true feelings. Critics can only be relied on if they give their honest thoughts, so they cannot change their opinions just because they feel pressured to do so.

Assignment 3

Write a movie review.

• • •

Step 1: Ask a relative or teacher to help you choose an age-appropriate movie you've never seen.

Step 2: While watching, take notes. How does the movie work? Is the story being told in order or does it jump around in time? Are there long takes/scenes or frequent cuts? Is the tone funny or dark and moody? Do the actors' performances match the tone? Does the soundtrack enhance the experience or detract from it? Is the ending supported by the beginning and middle?

Step 3: Come up with your overall opinion, and use examples from the movie to support that opinion. Then you can rank it out of five stars—one star being one of the worst movies you've seen, and five stars for one of the best.

Step 4: Now, in 450 words or less, write a brief plot summary about what happens in the movie before discussing your opinion and what you like and dislike about it.

For inspiration, or if you're feeling stuck, consider asking an adult to help you look up other movie reviews. You can find some written by TFK Kid Reporters at timeforkids.com.

● ● ●

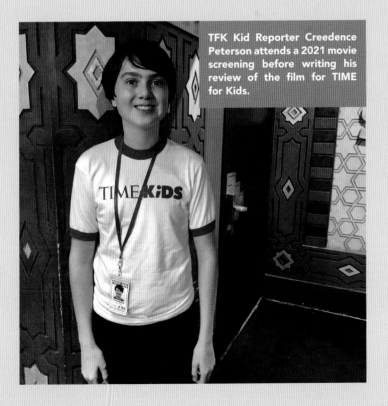

TFK Kid Reporter Creedence Peterson attends a 2021 movie screening before writing his review of the film for TIME for Kids.

CHAPTER 5

SPORTS

You don't have to be great at sports to be a great sports journalist.

Sports reporters cover all kinds of sports, from basketball and football to skateboarding and surfing, on both the amateur and professional level and from high school games to the Olympics.

Journalists who report on sports have a responsibility to tell their readers all of the important details from the events. These include the final score of the game or match and any important highlights. Perhaps a basketball player made a three-pointer with less than two seconds to go, causing the game to go into overtime. Maybe in a tennis match, a player served 20 aces after changing their technique, leading to a quick victory. Exciting details like these are what people who didn't get a chance to watch would want to know, and it's a sports reporter's job to make them feel like they were there for all of the action.

"I love sports journalism because it gives me the opportunity to cover some of the most exciting events in the world, while also getting to know the incredible athletes

In 2020, TFK Kid Reporter Zara Wierzbowski speaks with Maia and Alex Shibutani, Olympic medalists for ice dancing, in New York City.

who play in them," says Dominic Faria, a graduate student at Northwestern University's Medill School of Journalism, in Chicago.

Sports reporters have to think on their feet to provide commentary. In other words, these journalists need to be extremely knowledgeable about the history of the sport they're reporting on, the rules of the game, and the players on each team. They need to know who every team's star player is and who the new players are.

"Growing up in the San Francisco Bay Area, I always had a natural liking for all things sports," Faria says. "I enjoyed learning how games were played, who the players were, what motivated them, and tracking their stats. I remember spending lots of time listening to games and sports shows on the radio while on car rides with my mom and dad."

After playing his favorite sport—football—in high school, Faria joined the student newspaper at his college, the University of California, Davis, as a sports reporter, writing stories about student athletes. Later, Faria became the editor of the paper's sports section, assigning stories to reporters and then fact-checking and editing their stories. One of an editor's main responsibilities is to make sure stories read clearly and are accurate.

By giving commentary, sports journalists explain the

significance of the game in the context of the entire season and even in the history of a given sport.

> **Vocab word: COMMENTARY** is a verbal or written description, explanation, or opinion on a certain situation. In the context of sports, journalists provide commentary by weighing in during and after sports games with facts and opinions.

Explanations provided through commentary allow journalists to flag significant plays, injuries, and big scores for sports fans. Commentary also helps journalists build anticipation for future games, including playoffs.

"When I graduated from college, I started my own online publication and podcast show to continue writing and talking about sports," Faria says. "I learned how to set up my own website and produce a podcast, which isn't as easy as it looks."

Faria says he often invites friends to come on his podcast to talk about "the sports and the teams they care about." Voicing opinions on sports players and sports teams is the kind of casual yet informative commentary that broadcast sports journalists must know how to do on live TV or radio.

For this chapter's assignment, you will be given the opportunity to do breaking news or on-the-ground reporting. By conducting a postgame (after the game) interview, you'll have to prepare questions immediately and come up with a story on the fly.

Assignment 4

Report on a local sports game and conduct a postgame interview with an athlete or coach.

• • •

Step 1: Familiarize yourself with broadcast sports journalism by watching a sports game on TV. Take notes on the commentary and postgame analysis by the network's journalists.

Step 2: Choose a sporting event to attend in person, either at a local school or elsewhere in your community.

Step 3: Take detailed notes during the game. Ask the people around you questions about their impressions of the event. Remember to identify yourself as a journalist.

Step 4: After the game, ask an athlete or coach if they have time for a quick interview. Plan the questions you will ask. You might ask how they think the game went, or what their plans are for the rest of the season.

Inspired to learn more about sports journalism? There are many excellent sports writers whose work you can read, with an adult's permission. TIME for Kids often features articles written by TIME's senior sports correspondent Sean Gregory. He's interviewed many professional athletes and traveled the world reporting on major sporting events.

Faria says his favorite sports journalists are Marcus Thompson II, Mark Purdy, and Susan Slusser. "My goal is to one day become as good as they are at writing about the teams I love!" Faria says. Check out Thompson, Purdy, and Slusser's work by asking an adult to help you look for their stories online.

TFK Kid Reporter Ninis Twumasi speaks with commentator Lauren Shehadi, of the MLB Network, in 2024.

CHAPTER 6

FEATURES

Features journalists typically cover arts and culture stories as well as human interest pieces (stories that appeal to many readers and have a more emotional angle). Features take a closer look at a topic or person. A features writer might cover new exhibits at local museums and galleries; premieres of plays, operas, ballets, symphonies, and concerts; music, art, food, or craft festivals or fairs; and community events. Features also include profiles of people involved in these events.

Features articles are important because they entertain readers. They often use colorful and vivid storytelling to take readers into the topic they are covering. They might

In 2023, TFK Kid Reporter Harper Carroll smiles next to pastry chef Joanne Chang after interviewing her for a feature story.

describe the exciting flavors of an award-winning recipe or the funky sounds of a new band. Often, a features piece will be about just one person and will make readers feel like they have truly experienced the subject.

For this chapter's assignment, do research online with an adult or check out bulletin boards at your library or school administrative office for flyers that promote community events, performances, shows, or festivals. Check your school calendar—and calendars at local high schools and universities—to see if there's an upcoming theater, band, choir, or dance performance or even a comedy or talent show.

Community events might cost money to attend, but there are plenty of free arts and culture events on TV or online—just ask an adult for help. You can also visit a library and check out a book, CD, or DVD on any form of art.

Once you choose an event to attend, choose one person to interview who helped put it together, performed in it, or was otherwise important to its success. If you're checking out materials at the library or online, get creative with your sources. Consider interviewing your school arts or theater teacher.

Assignment 5

Write a question-and-answer (Q&A) piece.

• • •

A Q&A is essentially a transcribed interview with a single source. Your piece will need an intro. It should be 450 words or fewer. See the example below for how a Q&A piece should look, and then interview the person of your choice and do your own version!

EXAMPLE Q&A

TV news anchor and multimedia journalist Sarah Horbacewicz conducted her first interview in 2009 at age 11. Her source? Pop sensation Justin Bieber—who was, at that time, a Canadian teenager with a dream to make it big.

Horbacewicz's fifth-grade teacher had encouraged her and her classmates to apply for the TIME for Kids Kid Reporter program. Horbacewicz says she was a kid "who always wanted to be involved in everything," so she submitted her application and was ecstatic when she was selected.

Horbacewicz says she had so much fun as a TFK Kid Reporter, she didn't realize until years later how much it had changed her life. She got to attend a premiere of Disney's *The Princess and the Frog*, she went backstage and interviewed cast members of the *Lion King* musical on Broadway, and she even interviewed author Lois Lowry. Read on to find out what Horbacewicz has to say.

After being a TFK Kid Reporter, did you stay involved in journalism?

Horbacewicz: In high school, I joined the school paper immediately. We had a really big broadcast TV program, so we had lights and cameras. From the second I joined, I was immediately in. Then I became managing editor and editor in chief, and I started anchoring the morning announcements.

Did you plan to pursue journalism in college?

Horbacewicz: I started applying to journalism schools because I knew that's what I wanted to do. I ended up going to Ithaca College because they have a good communications school and I got a full-ride scholarship that focused on communications and community service.

What was your journalism career like in college?

Horbacewicz: I auditioned for 19 different [news] shows my freshman year. Eventually, I had a radio shift. It was at 5 a.m. In college, no one wants to do that shift, but it's when most people are listening to the radio on their drive to work. It's not glamorous, and that's when I realized journalism isn't necessarily glamorous.

What other journalism experiences did you have in college?

Horbacewicz: In college, I interned at NBC for the Winter Olympics and went to [South] Korea. I also interned in college for CBS News, and I was a runner for CNN for the Iowa caucuses for the 2020 election.

What's your current job like?
Horbacewicz: I wanted an experience that would challenge and help me grow as a journalist, so I moved to Little Rock, Arkansas. I'm the weekend news anchor on KTHV and a reporter for their prime-time show.

What has been one of your favorite memories from your time at KTHV?
Horbacewicz: We had a tornado here, and I remember talking to a family right after the storm, and they were crying because they were so grateful everyone was okay. So many people thanked us and said, "Because you were on the air, we knew to hide." I had people say, "You saved our lives." We told people where to get food and when the power was coming back on. People trust us—people trust us with their lives.

What advice do you have for young aspiring journalists?

Horbacewicz: If you're just a curious person, which I think a lot of kids are, just try it out. I think learning about people is super fun. Even if journalism isn't your thing, it's a good stepping stone to anything. It helps you learn how to communicate with people. Everyone has a different opinion on something. Everybody has a story, and every story is important.

CHAPTER 7

NEWS LITERACY

News literacy is the ability to sort fact from fiction and determine which sources are publishing informative and truthful news (as opposed to news that might be clouded by bias, opinion, or judgment).

Vocab word: A **BIAS** is a tendency in favor of or against one thing, one opinion, or one way of looking at things, typically in a way that seems unfair.

Tip: When conducting research, it's important to choose highly credible sources. Trustworthy sources include the official websites of museums, universities, government agencies, and highly reputable news organizations.

Vocab word: To **DEBUNK** a claim means to prove that it isn't true. To **DISPUTE** a claim means to question or express doubt about whether it is accurate or valid.

According to the News Literacy Project, there are five easy steps you can take to determine whether a source of information is reliable:

1. Search your source online and see how it's described. Do legitimate, trustworthy news organizations cite this source as credible? Or do they dispute or debunk claims made by your source?

2. Does your source have an ethics code? (An ethics code ensures that publications prioritize the truth and being honest.) Reputable news organizations often have a publicly viewable ethics code that can be found on their website's "about" or "contact" section.

3. Is your source clear about their reporting practices,

about who owns their organization, and about where their funding comes from? If so, are the reporting practices honest and respectable? If it's a news organization, do the journalists have editorial control (the ability to decide what to publish), or do the owners determine what stories do or do not get covered?

4. How does your source handle errors? A reputable news source owns up to its mistakes, explaining to readers how the mistakes occurred and what steps have been taken to correct them.

5. Use your own judgment. Does the source look, sound, and feel legitimate? Has your source conducted original reporting, or are they using information

from other websites? If something feels off, trust your gut.

If you're still unsure whether or not a source is trustworthy, ask a teacher, librarian, or other trusted adult for help.

TFK Kid Reporter Shaivi Moparthi speaks with Vanessa E. Wyche, director of NASA's Johnson Space Center, in 2022.

CHAPTER 8

NOTABLE JOURNALISTS THROUGHOUT HISTORY

From professional reporters at national newspapers and television news outlets to student reporters working for their high school or college newspapers, journalists of all ages have made huge differences in their communities—and their countries—throughout history.

NELLIE BLY

Let's leap back nearly 140 years to the 1880s, when female reporter Nellie Bly began her career as an investigative journalist—a profession that, up until then, had been dominated by men. One of Bly's biggest stories was inspired by the 1872 French novel *Around the World in Eighty Days*,

by Jules Verne. On November 14, 1889, Bly—then a reporter at the *New York World* newspaper—began her investigation to see if she could break the travel record established in the novel by completing a 25,000-mile journey around the world in less than 80 days. The airplane had not yet been invented, so Bly had to travel exclusively by boat (and became very seasick during her first few days on board). Yet she successfully completed the journey in a record-breaking 72 days, traveling to places such as Sri Lanka, China, and Japan.

BOB WOODWARD & CARL BERNSTEIN

In the 1970s, *Washington Post* reporters Bob Woodward (right) and Carl Bernstein (left) published a series of investigative stories that were so important and shocking that they led to the resignation of the president of the United States, Richard Nixon. Woodward and Bernstein exposed the Watergate conspiracy to the public. They started by investigating a burglary at Democratic National Committee Headquarters, at the Watergate building complex, in Washington, DC. That led to an investigation of how Nixon and members of his reelection committee carried out acts of political interference and then conspired to cover them up. Because of Woodward and Bernstein's stories and the ensuing presidential resignation, American politics were never the same. The scandal changed the way many Americans viewed government officials and the president, causing citizens to be much less trusting of their leaders.

CHRISTIANE AMANPOUR

In the 1980s, Christiane Amanpour graduated from the University of Rhode Island with a degree in journalism and began her career in broadcast news, working first for NBC and then for CNN, ABC, and PBS news. Since 2009,

Amanpour has had her own TV news programs, and she is well-known for her thoughtful, in-depth interviews with world leaders and celebrities. Amanpour has consistently shown up at the front lines of the biggest world events, from natural disasters to elections, and has used her fame as a well-known journalist to advocate for human rights and journalists' rights.

THEO BAKER

In 2022 (not so long ago!), Stanford college student Theo Baker published the first of more than a dozen investigative stories focused on neuroscientist and Stanford president Marc Tessier-Lavigne. Baker's reporting revealed that Tessier-Lavigne had published scientific research containing errors and had run labs with a high amount of data manipulation (meaning the data was purposely changed to produce inaccurate conclusions). After Baker's stories were published, Tessier-Lavigne stepped down as Stanford president, and Baker became the youngest person ever to win a George Polk Award, at just 18 years old. The George Polk Award is one of the highest honors in journalism. Previous recipients include Bob Woodward, Carl Bernstein, and Christiane Amanpour. Baker showed that journalists of all ages can make a difference through hard work and a commitment to pursuing the truth.

CHAPTER 9

GO FORTH!

You've learned about famous journalists who have changed the world, and now you know how to look for and write stories like those authored by Nellie Bly and Theo Baker. Your voice, your perspective, and your opinions matter. You can make a change in your community. You're ready to put what you've learned into practice.

What now? It's time to find a story that calls to you! Chances are you won't have to go very far to find inspiration.

Where should you look for stories?

In your school! Is there a science fair, fundraiser, dance, sports game, or big assignment coming up? Events and activities are great subjects to write about. You can help inform your classmates about events they should have on their calendar. If it's a dance, does it cost money to attend? If it's a game, whom will your school be competing against? If it's a big assignment, when is it due? These are all important questions to ask that will lead to answers your readers want to know.

Look in your community! New businesses like restaurants, clothing stores, bookstores, and cafés are always opening up. Write about a new business in your town, review a new ice-cream shop, or interview a store owner

for a Q&A piece. Make sure you take detailed notes when you visit the business to set the scene for readers. How is the business decorated? How does it smell? What sounds do you hear? Were you welcomed when you walked in? Was it a memorable experience? If it's a review, make sure to express your own opinion fairly and honestly to readers. Be sure to incorporate quotes from interviews you conduct with the business owner, employees, and customers, as well as details about your experience.

TFK Kid Reporter Via Ryerson interviews Dr. Eugenia South—who lives and works in Via's hometown of Philadelphia, Pennsylvania—in 2021.

Look inside your own home! (Yes, there are stories to be told in your home right this very second.) Choose someone you live with—it could be a parent, grandparent, sibling, cousin, or anyone else in your home—and profile them. What is a profile? It's an in-depth story of someone's life as told by that person and by people who know them well. For instance, if you were to interview a parent, make sure to ask them about their childhood, their favorite memories, and their hopes for the future. Your readers will want to know when and where your profile subject was born, where they went to school, what they do for work, and what hobbies they have. You should also interview other people who know your interview subject well, such as their family members, friends, or coworkers, to get different perspectives on your subject's personality, likes, and dislikes. Your goal is to paint as detailed and accurate a picture of your subject as possible for readers who might not know them.

It's time to apply what you've learned in this book by practicing good journalism habits. That means sorting fact from fiction, conducting interviews, being honest with your readers, and giving a complete, detailed, accurate picture of the person, place, or event at the heart of your story.

Have you completed a story that you're proud of? Consider asking a parent, teacher, or guardian to help you send it to the TIME for Kids editors, at tfkeditors@time.com. Visit timeforkids.com for story prompts and submission details, as well as for the chance to read work from other junior journalists and make your own press badge.

What stories will you tell?

BIBLIOGRAPHY

• • •

IDA B. WELLS

Walker, Malea. "Ida B. Wells and the Activism of Investigative Journalism." Library of Congress Blogs. February 12, 2020. https://blogs.loc.gov/headlinesandheroes/2020/02/ida-b-wells-and-the-activism-of-investigative-journalism/.

NELLIE BLY

"Around the World in Eighty Days." Britannica. Last modified January 14, 2024. https://www.britannica.com/topic/Around-the-World-in-Eighty-Days-by-Verne.

Lawson, Pace. "Nellie Bly: Around the World." Heinz History Center. https://www.heinzhistorycenter.org/learn/women-forging-the-way/nellie-bly-around-the-world/.

Norwood, Arlisha R., and Mariana Brandman. "Nellie Bly." National Women's History Museum. https://www.womenshistory.org/education-resources/biographies/nellie-bly-0.

WOODWARD & BERNSTEIN

"Bob Woodward and Carl Bernstein: An Inventory of Their Watergate Papers at the Harry Ransom Center." Harry Ransom Center. https://norman.hrc.utexas.edu/fasearch/findingAid.cfm?eadid=00365.

"Watergate Scandal." History.com. Last modified October 18, 2023. https://www.history.com/topics/1970s/watergate.

"Watergate Scandal: Watergate Trial and Aftermath." Britannica. Last modified February 4, 2024. https://www.britannica.com/event/Watergate-Scandal/Watergate-trial-and-aftermath.

CHRISTIANE AMANPOUR

"Christiane Amanpour." Britannica. Last modified March 5, 2024. https://www.britannica.com/biography/Christiane-Amanpour.

"Christiane Amanpour: Chief International Anchor." CNN. https://www.cnn.com/profiles/christiane-amanpour-profile#about.

THEO BAKER

Bonos, Lisa. "Meet the Student Who Helped Boot the President of Stanford." *Washington Post*, July 28, 2023. https://www.washingtonpost.com/media/2023/07/28/theo-baker-stanford-president-tessier-lavigne/.

Dalva, Cassidy. "Daily Wins Polk Award, First for an Independent, Student-Run Newspaper." *Stanford Daily*, February 20, 2023. https://stanforddaily.com/2023/02/20/daily-staffer-wins-polk-award-first-for-an-independent-student-run-newspaper/.

• • •